Junctions of the Heart

Volume Three of Awakening
My Sleeping Poetess

by

Sandra Ann Humphreys

PublishAmerica
Baltimore

First printing

PublishAmerica has allowed this work to remain exactly as the author intended, verbatim, without editorial input.

Softcover 9781451295047
PUBLISHED BY PUBLISHAMERICA, LLLP
www.publishamerica.com
Baltimore

Printed in the United States of America

KEEP ON GOING
c 2011

Even though the tears of frustration fall

sometimes

I pick myself up & say

just keep on going

I fail, I win, I lose

But once again, I keep on going

Bleakest shots of reality

Still cause my heart to dream

And I slowly drift away

But I turn around once more

And keep on going

To my next step

I keep on going

A DATE
c 1995

A party

People

A beer

A laugh

Drunkenness

A rape

Trauma

Pain

Anguish

Talking

Sharing

Growing

Healing

A friend

A date

A party

People

A beer

A laugh

Drunkenness

A rape

DO YOU REMEMBER
c 2002

Do you remember how much I loved you?

When you first moved into my heart

I remembered how I loved you

Denying that it was wrong

And every reason I cared for you was wrong

And every wrong reason

Anytime, any minute, anywhere

How my life changed from bad to worse

With the times we shared

I wanted to tell you I loved the Lord

But my brain was a mess and

All in the memory of great pain

But Jesus rescued me

And after years I feel some gain

Once more

Forgiveness being the key to unshackle my chains

So all that is to be remembered

Is a life rescued from pains of a distorted brain

The Lord does not always agree with

My sacrifice because he would prefer obedience

In my repair

CHOICES BY SANDY

God gives us a choice when he presents us with an opportunity...or when He allows us to suffer.

We can decide to take up the opportunity or let it pass.

When He allows us to suffer, we either do things the way the world would (blame others, blame God, hate others, hate God etc. or try to fix things ourselves, without praying or being obedient to the scriptures), or do the will of the Lord, which pleases God.

To please God, we must turn to praying, praising Him and thanking Him in all our circumstances whether pleasant or painful, (longsuffering which builds character).

If it is God's decision to allow us pain, then we must trust him. He knows what to do and where to lead us because of it.

God gives us strength to be successful at what he wants us to be successful at or accomplish—not necessarily what we want to be successful at or accomplish.

He put us on this earth to serve him...and that is our main purpose & opportunity for living.

The more we are filled with God's purpose (opportunity to serve Him and please Him)—the more our desire to do evil lessons, especially through prayer, in praise of Him and thanking him for all the things in our lives we appreciate. Then we are blessed on earth & rewarded further still with eternal life, in Heaven...

Life is worth it because when we do get to Heaven we'll find true love because Jesus had no reason to come to earth except for his love for us.

As my life continues I have become a more loving, caring, compromising, understanding and less judgemental Christian and I have given up quarrel for quiet.

I am accountable to God, not only in the sight of Him but also in the sight of man.

The more I give the more I am able to give (investing rather than borrowing).

If there is anything in nature or creation that you find enjoyable, or wonderful here on earth, just imagine what Heaven will be like...

My Christian walk is a constant challenge do the right thing and allow the Lord to keep me balanced—to walk when it is time to walk & wait when it is time to wait. I must give God the time to respond and not to rush things on my own.

I FACE IT
c 1987

Once in a while
A spark does flicker showing some light
In my lonely existence
of brain pain
But it soon dies down
Without a substance to burn
Someone sparked my day
And caused interest
But not in God`s plan I guess
We were not looking for each other
So I face it
It could have been wrong and deceitful
But I believe in goodness
Thank you God for your protection
But will the wall ever break down
The wall that just stands there
You know my troubles and my thoughts
You know my sadness and pain
And the long journey back to being myself again
I trust you will work it out
With all the love to go around
I feel faint
Why does it always end there

WITH YOU TONIGHT
c 2011

It`s when you love to hold me
A special time begins
I want to hold you back
But wait cause were just friends

I`ve felt the touch of another
That made me want to cry
But the needs I have inside of me
You gently satisfy

I`ll never stop talking to you
Sweet joy I feel with humble pride
I`m always happy to be with you
And sit down by your side

Sweet bliss for me in your finger tips
The way you listen and the way you share
From the moment I see your face again
I know that you still care

My heart says don`t let go
Next to you is a good place to stay
To share what`s meant to be
Not a hurting yesterday

SPENDING TIME TOGETHER
c 2011

The more I see you the more I smile
Inside and out
And connecting is great
I feel a bond beginning
I`ve heard of really getting to know someone
And I am getting to know many
I`m keeping a natural pace, a happy place
I am more responsible
I`m growing up inside
It`s true
No rushing, just maintaining my boundaries
And my love for God
You help me with your stunningly fresh friendship
I hope you understand

ALL MY DAYS NOW
c 1999

As I drive on into life
I`m triggered into the past
Once again only to leave it there, move on then let it go
Reaching out to make new waves
In my reality ocean
Without so much hardship
Of emotion
Pleased to let life take its course
Relaxed, I let it flourish
As I look away from death
And its piercing eyes
Looking for a loved one to talk to
Staring as I travel in silence
To soft, warm, foaming oceans
Praying, and listening for clues
Of a joyful expression
Loving God in all my days
In all my ways

WHATEVER
c 2011

Whatever you say, whatever you do
You'll find God's love is the only love that's true
If you forgive me and I forgive you
All that's left is a little color blue

God takes my pain and lessens it
Or makes it go away
So I'm no longer feeling down
And go along my way

Now whatever failing mental health I have
I look into the light
I find a peace I never knew
And God makes it alright

I thought you were the man for me
God knew so much better
He was trying to peel me away from you
As I wrote my final unlovely love letter

I spent five years too long
In trying to make it work out
And straying away from you Lord
With many a scream and shout

Thanks again for rescuing me
Father in Heaven
Now I'm happy with
The new friendships I've been given

MOTHER: A FRIENDSHIP
C 1984

Do I dare separate a friendship
I feel the love
It is worth it to keep it
As I am still on my own
The day I have not loved you I have never known
Even with the anger and pain
Would you ever choose
Me over the past?
How could you lose
Can you still praise the Lord even if I don't sing along
Even a song to poet a love grown up
A memory I have of you holding me as a child
A day to hold your hand again
To see you smile again
You and I have paid our dues and
Walked that lonely mile in each others' shoes
Always think of me as that little girl who loves you still
And as the friend who will always be of yours

THE RISING AND FALLING OF SHAME AND PRIDE
c 2011

Success is an immeasurable value sometimes
Surrounded by the days of thunder that bathe the flower petals
and sometimes drown the very young life of a bud
The waterfall that spreads to streams to rivers to oceans
Over rocks and craggy hills
Eternally returning to sky to rain and running water infinite
Progression: even in a twisted turmoil there are some things that
can remain grounded: values
Weather the storm when it is all that there is for now
Your reward is your own constant
Devotion and obedience
Security is found in constant learning and discovery, adventure
and opportunity to become healthy again
That constant in the Love of God leading us somewhere
To our eternal life the comfort knowing it

MAKE A JOYFUL SOUND
c 1994

Make a joyful sound
Unto our gracious Lord
Rejoicing all our faith in Him
By singing of His word

My saviour came into my heart
To accept Him I am saved
And in God's Holy book of life
You'll find my name engraved

No more will I be lost
And looking all around
But by faith in God alone
I know I have been found

Now my life is filled with joy
Through fellowship with Him
And with my Born-again Christian friends around
My new life does begin

So I make a joyful sound
Unto a loving God
Rejoicing in His love and grace
By singing every word

WITH A LITTLE HEART
c 1990

With a little heart I'm speaking
With effort in direction right
It's the love of God I'm seeking
To help me sleep tonight

Me and my voice we will rejoice
Yesterday and I are not to blame
It seems that there was not much choice
But the love of God remains the same

Tomorrow and I we have hope
Lord guard my brain against insane
But it's still possible to cope
Even thought there is still much pain

I'm thankful that God's my better life
He helps me to begin
To work out the bitter strife
And leave behind the efforts due to sin

LADY LUCK
c 1984

Lady, lady luck in store
Return to me from
Your daydreams once more
You haven't been my friend you see
So could you try just once for me
I'm feeling blue
And sit alone
Twice today I wished you'd phoned
Haven't you missed me
Lady with the news
Or have I enlisted
In the army of the blues
Please don't leave me
Like this again
For I'll be lonely
If not your friend

KING OF HEARTS
c 2000

A true heart beats for God above
Just one true love
It understands life's cold hearts
And tries to bring them warmth
Changing hearts need love
A true heart understands
And whispers the love message of Jesus
Even though the head is sometimes
Thoughtless, or insane
The king of hearts has a true love to heal
The pain of indecision and hurting souls
Jesus is the king of hearts
And he plays my hand when I cannot
When my mind is being tortured and the Beast is trying to eat my brain
He is the king of hearts
When I fear loneliness and lose direction
He is the way, the truth and the life

JUNCTIONS OF THE HEART
c 2011

While we keep in touch where do we meet
Somewhere on the street
When again will we embrace
Certainly not in outer space
Once this notion gets a hold of me
Junctions of the heart will set us free
You are no stranger to my eyes
When we meet again as a surprise
I shall not look, but let God guide
I shall not fear, He's by my side
Whenever, wherever meeting at a junction
Where God prepares us to newly function
Now or in Heaven it will be great
If I see you now or at the pearly gate

THE GRAND MANIPULATION
c 2011

Am I missing out on love
Or has all its ever been was bad advice through manipulation and torture
What I mistook for love
Love had a bad reputation in my growing up house
My mind cannot embrace the
torment I am incurring
My past experiences just confuse me if I'm triggered to think about them
Oh praise the Lord for his helping me to move on and then let go
Moving on is O.K. but getting back to being myself again still has an engine
*   and only works when I can work things out in my head*
I try to forgive you Lord because most times I still don't understand why I
*   had to go through it all*
And have to continue feeling taken

EFFECTIVE COPING
c 2011

When the past is too difficult to accept I turn to effective healing—coping—healing
It never gave me hope for the future
As I constantly try to forgive myself and dealing with that part of my life
that overwhelms me
The present I can deal with one hour at a time
Constantly questioning my mental health
But I believe there is reward for doing right
And punishment for doing wrong
And God sees fit to take care of it himself
We all must pray for effective coping mechanisms such as love which can be
a more effective healer than time and both together truly must heal
Heartache and chronic sorrow
for a whirlwind of a life
Best be on my way now
And accept love overcoming the pain

ON HEALING
c 1997

Many the moment of trial and error
Many the torment and I the bearer
Sun and moon, in spite it seems
Relieve the treachery of my past dreams

Freedom is slow, but sure to come
In healing bounds of one lump sum
Lord above, you are here
You see my pain, I shed a tear

Master, master, your love is real
I know it by the way I feel
Dear Lord I'm glad you gave
A light to see, my life to save

Let go of me oh body sin
Let God's true love have growth within
I want real love, and feel less pain
So all that's left is love to gain

INKDOM
c 2002

With flow thru ink
I use my pen
To find some peace
I'm writing again

I put it down
On paper a feeling
My mind confused
Sometimes stays reeling

You to me
My mind you stole
I write that down
Then I'm in control

My pen and ink
Its kingdom folly
Thoughts out of control
Not light or jolly

I gave out what I knew as love
Love not real anyways
Discoveries made over many years
All through my isolated days

SHARING
c 1983

Treacherous, continued path of emotion
Valuable contained emotion
With whom can I share love and devotion to God
When will we win and get to go on
Together
If he wants it
He has to be sure of it
The love he has for God
Friendship first
I have to give it back:
The Love I possess for the Lord
Effortless continual peace that passes understanding
Given by God
We'll contain it
Join and relate on an exceptional level
Commitment—the freedom to commit

Co-operate with Jesus by practicing love & trusting God more, also forgiving & being grateful for His love & forgiveness of me because lack of forgiveness means lack of love in my heart, mind, body, and soul for others and God.

Manage the devil (by practicing forgiveness)

Cope with life (by _trusting God more by looking for his love & affirming it to myself fully_ then _practice_ forgetting the painful memories and move on to future hopes & dreams)

WHEN YOU LISTEN TO COUNTRY MUSIC YOU HAVE TO BE UNDER ITS SPELL.
SANDRA ANN HUMPHREYS
c 2011

PAIN
c 2011

Does pain equate with good feelings
Does my mind trick me
And make me think the pain feels good
And the absence of pain feels lonely
Is it the pain that makes me feel good
If I recognize it is pain I flee
But I do not lie to my own mind
To protect myself from the pain of loneliness anymore

PEACE
c 1983

God, the master of the scenery

Creation puts the puzzle into perspective

Illuminating the glory of man, animals, mountains, valleys, trees, plants, wind & weather

A beautiful whimsical reality

This is peace, peace of mind

Leaving endless traces

But the moment it takes to say peace

Is the only moment there is peace

Because everything that lead to it will ultimately lead away from it

So for all it's worth, I say peace, peace for all its humble & mighty directions

HELLO.
c 1994

Tracing a trail, or following a patternless clue

What is it ultimately that you are trying to place into my brain
For a reaction of your selfishness...

Trial & error to the demise of my sanity or my truth, left with no power
or froth...

Whatever he speaks, he is of the nourishment of the lack of bread

Equally my trauma resisted his attempt to resolve his guilt

Try me again...

HE FORGIVES THAT SONG
c 1994

Today, God sent this rainy sky
Its darkness here this morning
I felt refreshed by misty breeze
The rain brought without warning

The gentle swish as cars went by
Held my closeness to the past
Reminding me of large downpours
I wished would last and last

Just as rain can clear a road
Of tiny loose debris
The rain's symbolic of brand new life
And how it set me free

And now I'm glad I realized
It was God who held the key
And like new rain, He cleared my slate
And forgave me constantly

So now I tell Him I'm aware
When I've done something wrong
And in my prayer He knew I asked him to
So He forgave that song

The rainy hours felt good today
They brought His lasting love
So I am never sad or blue
About rain from up above

FINALLY FORGIVEN
c 2011 Sandra Ann Humphreys

I finally feel free of the past and have forgiven

Everything and everyone I can

Including myself

And am quicker to forgive

And choose quiet and calm

Over calamity

Although there are little spurts

Of uncertainty

And confusion

I cannot go on blaming or searching for retribution

I may never receive

But God comforts me

He loosens chains

That bind me now and then

When Satan has his way

I am free to love as a beginner

Even though I've loved the Lord all along

Please teach me to be filled with the Holy Spirit

And accept Him as mine

THE LINES ON YOUR FACE
c 2011 Kempenfest Barrie, Ontario
by Sandra Ann Humphreys

The little tuft of beard
In the middle of your chin
Just cannot disguise the lines on your face
That completely draw me in

You seem like such a gentle type
You let me get my way
I've loved all your performances
I've watched so carefully

I cannot find the words
As you make me feel so much
Your arm around my shoulder photo
With an endearing kind of touch

The four or five times we've met
I just cannot understand
My admiration feelings
Watching you inside the band

The lines on your face
Kindly moulded there by God
I seek my refuge inside of them
Getting ready to applaud

I don't wish to bother you
But a coffee would be nice
To discover more about you
And maybe break the ice

It wouldn't be nice
To steal your heart away
I know you must be happy
And I'd like you to stay that way

But the lines on your face
Are somehow matching mine
So I leave it all up to God
Who will show his love divine

My ears remember stories
My eyes saw long ago
I don't know if you'll remember me
But I'm sure of what I know

MY SHANIA KITTY-CAT MY PET PASSED AWAY JULY 17TH AT 7:07 P.M. I LOOKED AFTER HER FOR 17 YEARS AFTER TAKING HER IN AS A STRAY

Dedicated to our special bond Me & Shania kitty-cat

YOUR EVERYWHERE I TURN
c 2011 Sandra Ann Humphreys

You're everywhere I turn
You purr and then you smile
I pick you up & cuddle you
And rock you for a while

Thank you for your kisses
As I tucked you in nite-nite
I miss you being next to me
Now that you are gone from site

I miss your presence immensely
I feel you're gone so much
I just want to pet your fur
As you give me a gentle paw touch

I miss you in the daytime
I miss you all nite long
You've been a precious kitty-friend to me
So I sing your kitty song

I know that you're in Heaven
Doesn't mean I won't always miss you
Say hi to everybody up there
And remember I love you

I love you more today than I did yesterday
And I'll love you more tomorrow than I do today
I'll hold you precious in my heart
Even though you're gone away

Love Mommy

YOUR EYES SO GREEN
c 2006 Sandra Ann Humphreys March 04/07
Barrie, On

CHORUS
When he stayed out so late at nite
Loving him didn't seem so right
He turned around and said good-bye
Before I had a chance to cry
But God sent me your eyes so green
And I don't fear days-in-between
I always wanted someone true
Because the dark turned deepest blue

VERSE 1
You helped me up, I felt alive
Got over him and still survived
In this world so full of lies
Everyone's got alibis
But your green eyes so full of light
Make my future seem so bright

MUSIC SOLO

VERSE 2
I never thought I'd feel alone
And needed someone on the phone
So out of touch I seemed to be
Then God sent me your eyes so green
Now suddenly it feels so right
I'm never lonely dark at night

BRIDGE

Sharing love with you is bliss
I love you with a hug and kiss
I feel like I've just passed the test
Cause you true love just feels the best

REPEAT CHORUS

WAIT ON THE LORD
by Sandra Ann Humphreys c 2010

I wait, & I wait

Time is not ready for me

Sincere as it is

The seconds & minutes

Do not pass so swiftly

Now

As I wait & I wait

Wondering pausing

Thinking

No less does it change

For time tells on me

It does not change me

Only Jesus can

TOUGH ON US
c 2010 Sandra Ann Humphreys

You know it's tough on me
Looking for a gentle man
And I know it's tough on you
Trying to love all over again

But somehow it's worth trying
To find that peace of mind
And somehow stop the crying
And leave the past behind

Never to be easy
Or just plain go away
But the trials we've learned to deal with
Keep us present in today

Still you my darling angel
May be just a darling man
A complex combination
Of God's all perfect plan

I need your hugs and kisses
And I need you in my life
I'll pledge my vows and live the dream
As a God-fearing gentle wife

Someday someone special will find me
And he'll treat me like a queen
And take me to that special place
Where I have never been

THE PAIN WE MUST WORK THROUGH
by Sandra Ann Humphreys c 2009 May

Long live past discouragements in my heart for you now

Below the level of love

Seeing you would be the highlight of my life

Even better to hold your hand

To hold past the discouragements in my heart for me

Your beauty shines through like the blizzard of a white storm

Considered that it is joy for me to behold the droplets of pain wishing that I could be the cure

Loving you in many senses but not finding you in the light

Although it would be a long shot I have always gone for the underdog

You may need peace of mind alone for a true picture of love

The Lord in your heart and the profession of truth

May God richly bless your heart in the love I hold for you in mine

Although we've never met I keep you burning in the fire of my heart as you keep me warm on the coldest of nights

My lonely existence beats my heart one more night

Waiting for someone to spend the nights close and quiet

PASS THE SUGAR
c 2009 October 25th/09 Sandra Ann Humphreys
Barrie, Ontario

Pass the sugar, sugar

It's still just morning time

We've got all day

Today

To make our bodies rhyme

Pass the sugar, love

I love you too

What a great beginning

For the promises we've made

With two diamond bands

No more lonely one night stands

Love has picked us up

And left it where it lands

Maybe we're not perfect

But perfecting love will be

A pleasant Godly lifestyle

Meant for you and me

I WANT TO HEAR THREE WORDS
by Sandra Ann Humphreys c 2006

(chorus)
I may get down
But life goes on
Until I hear from you again
My life's a lonely one

(verse 1)
I want to hear three words
Those words are "I Love You!"
I want to be beside you
When the sun meets morning dew

(verse 2)
I'm so lonely cause you're gone away
But I know you don't want to be
I hope you miss me like I miss you
When you're not here with me

(verse 3)
I hope love's in our future
By the simple things we've done
We've shared each other's feelings
And we've had a lot of fun

(chorus)

(bridge)
I don't believe love's casual
Love's not just an affair
We need our blessing from above
And I need to know you're there

(verse 4)
Somehow I keep on praying
I won't be all alone
With only friends and family
To talk to on the phone

(repeat chorus)

SOMEONE TO HOLD
c 2011 Sandra Ann Humphreys

All I'm doing is

Praying for someone to hold

Praying in the darkness

Praying in the light

All I'm doing is

Praying for someone tonight

A smile to greet—bonjour

My hand to kiss—enchante

All I am doing is praying

For someone to hug

Praying in the darkness

Praying in the light

Praying that someone

Will make it right

Someone so happy

Someone so bold

All I'm doing is praying for someone to hold

HOSPITAL BLUES
c Sandra Ann Humphreys

Waiting to get out tomorrow but tomorrow never comes

We're a bunch of waiting souls

Starting out today one step at a time toward another goal

Daily taking what good we find

And trying to leave yesterday behind

It would be easy if so much didn't happen

And it would be easy if there was not so much pain

And it would be easier if I didn't have to bear it all those years

NOT TOO OLD
c 1994 Sandra Ann Humphreys

I tied my shoes when I was small
Some things I wish I didn't recall
That happened in the unfinished house on the hill
Dad built sometime near fall

When we lived there
God's presence could be felt
All of us had pillows to lay our heads upon
But His love is why we knelt

I don't know what happened
But the house dad built was sold
Like a blur our family separated
Leaving many bad memories to hold

I had the spark of interest
The desire to serve the Lord
I still have few world advantages
But God's love I can afford

So much has changed with healing
My heart sees love more clearly
God's plan for me is working out
Christ's love I hold more dearly

But I'm still young in Jesus
It's better the more I forgive
But I pray I'm not old to thank Him
My life on earth to live

FAMILY
c Sandra Ann Humphreys

Dear unhappy ones…
Please be happy…
You share some joy and sometimes have some fun for me
I miss it sometimes as I teary glow
Right up to the ceiling
I wish you all much success
I've thought of you kindly but I bet you disappear
Especially taking care of my blue thoughts
Two breaks to make one family!
What makes us strong enough to cope
Where wondering I find myself sometimes
Long away from advice to be taken
Foggy and full of pain
In a smile, a thoughtful note, or card, or gift
Let's count our blessings as we are separated now

MY NEIGHBOURHOOD
(POPLAR HILLS)
c 2011

He broke our Moto-ski so who pays? His dad? or us?

He cut through our back yard

Mom was generous but he took her for a ride in swimming pledges

Miles for Millions when Carolyn was late and it rained and we could go no further than a mile in squishy shoes

The new neighbourhood boy Glori got to first

The neighbours took us to church on Sundays but sometimes I called Dad to pick me up & we never talked, he just nervously looked around

Swimming @ 6 a.m. and getting numb Septembers with Mom

We were all pizza people & I worked there too & got abused by a driver

The MacLauchlan's house was the best on Halloween and she bribed me with 25 cents to dig up a tree for her back yard

The school bus dad converted into a camper to go to Florida in & Pop called me "Suzi Sunshine" and Raymond "Yogi" & Cookie learned to walk in it

Dad's drug addict friend who slept with his wife (mom) & caused my parents' break-up and raped his daughter (me) & gave me hallucinogenic drugs, alcohol, marijuana and cigarettes

Dad's Simcoe Paving, Asphalt services, and friendly snow removal

Bicycles, mini-bikes and motorcycles at our house

Mini skis for Christmas to use at the Golf Course

Our house became the party house—The Rolling Stones and Frank Zappa

Basketball was my forte and the boys said I was too good to play hockey with them & Sherri stole my skates

My best friend and my Mom made fun of me as I started menstruating & then she stole my mother from me

Liz still has the K.F.C. chicken coating mix recipe

Reggie always needed a dollar's worth of gas to take us to school—he painted the basement black for posters & strobe lights

I fell asleep on the rug to the radio on the Hi-fi
The Osmond's and the Jackson Five were all the rage for my age
Water fights—buckets of water throughout the house left for Mom to clean
I loved to harmonize to Neil Diamond but Marion said "you can't do
    that!" & Jo-Helen had the doughnuts for information about Reggie
Couchiching Beach Park & Bass Lake Park were the places to go in the summer
We pitched the tent in our back yard & and slept in Dad's bus-camper

I'M TAKING BACK MY LIFE
c 2004

When your lover thinks
Nothing is forbidden
He's not really there for you
And the Bible says that you're backslidden

Nobody will respect you
When you act like this
His gratification was his only concern
And it started with just a kiss

Now I'm taking back my life
And changing all the lies I was told
About a casual look on life
When my abusers were so bold

I have to take a stand in life
Now that I found out all the news
I finally found out the truth in life
That I have the right to choose

I learned that there are boundaries
I don't allow those to cross
They must respect my wishes
Even though much time was lost

Thank you Lord for showing me
How you can turn around
A life full of love gone wrong
And plant my feet back on the ground

God's Genuine Love is the "Proof" in a combination of—

communication of knowledge and feelings, care, affection, delight, commitment, trust, positive attention, respect, accountability, and responsibility for your own feelings, successes, and joys with His help

THANK YOU LORD
c 2009

Thanks to you Lord
I can have a best friend
And thanks to you Lord
I can be one in the end

Sometimes the summer heat
Makes our remarks
The hurtful words
That break our hearts

And even though our towns
Are miles and miles apart
We can still be friends
And hug each other's heart

Please Lord continue to stay
By each other's side
Summer, winter, spring, and fall
And always be our guide

Let what stands between us
Never tear us apart
And if it does dear Lord
Let us make a brand new start

God makes His plan for me
Clearer every day
And so it helps my being
To get down on my knees and pray

Thanks to you Lord
I can have a best friend
And thanks to you Lord
I can be one in the end

WHAT IS DIVORCE?
c 1983

I love you mother, I love you father
Making myself an individual has not been easy without your help and I
don't always understand circumstances beyond my control or without your guidance.
For the most part the older I get, the more I only want to miss and set my
heart to grow fonder of you.
A love that has crowded and inconvenienced my soul exists and my
interpretations have not been my own, or yours. These are what a parent
does not give to me, but take a way as I a single unit they do it dually &
separately tearing me apart at the seams.
Too many things still join divorced people especially the anger and hatred.
They are freer to live & love others than the children and do not want to
face obligations and responsibilities to those who love them. At times this is
welcome at other times it is an overwhelming burden.

BLACK & WHITE
c 2009

How colourful
Everything is now
How sharp is the pain
All sunshine and no rain
Why can't we go back to the
Simple pleasures
To black and white
And just try to remain
Calm
Me loving my family
And my family loving me
Let us try to forget
All the light
And just go back
To black and white
Let us try to forget
All the light
And go back
To black and white

JUST LIKE ME
c 1985

One more time my pain will pass
Why does this keep repeating
I don't know whether to
Go forward or start retreating

Sweet poisonous honey
With just a look you pierce
Into young girls eyes
While your touch is forever fierce

You left me crushed
And stumbling for the light
At the age of 12
Afraid of the night

What a prey so innocent
What a course mine was to follow
In all my pain and sorrow
For so many years in which to wallow

The pain of your sting
Not lying of your deceit
Your sincerity in deadly play
I did not wish to greet

As simply drinking water
The young girls who should've been free
Received much negativity like yours
Are meant to be just like me

SHARING
c 1983

Treacherous, contained emotion
Valuable contained emotion
With whom can I share God's love and devotion
When will I win and get to go on with it
He wants it…but I am not sure
Now I have to be sure of it
Before I was not informed
I have to give it effort
He has to see the light
He has to let me in
Does he want to be my best friend?
He has to prove it…
I must winter him, summer him, into the fall and spring
I am worth the wait
After all…I've been waiting for so long
Our souls must be settled and defined not wavy and
undefined

OOH...GOODNESS
c 1984

Tall & powerful your structure rests
But all of God's glory must be put to the tests
Why is there a space so mighty
For my tender words so soft and flighty
Something about you aggresses my need
For lack of sophistication, I just don't want the deed
Should I speak of want, need, or desire
Should I hope to arouse a spark or fire
Ooh, goodness you've touched my senseless heart
Now I forbid to be apart
You used my innocent heart's caress
For your selfish gain and my distress
I still remember thoughts of you
But all with senseless pain
I'm so tired of being used help me Lord with my refrain
I really don't know what to do
Everything's so wrong what else is new

TOMORROW
c 1984

Dilly, dally, daily, the calculative error
To me, to you, I wonder oh where
This day is not lost, because I have not yet spoken
It seems that when I do, everything in my heart gets broken
Tomorrow where will I awake
A one-sided affair will cause my heart to break
Is this a beginning, the end, no longer do I care
What's love?
All I ever know is a broken heart, whenever I decide to share
All my aces are gone
I'm lost in this nothingness, my heart is all alone
No one will tell me what I'm doing wrong
Do they think I want to sing this song
Lord all I know is to hold on tight
To your love I know tonight
I'm in the wrong place, I must be with the wrong friends
I don't want to go to Heaven before this all ends
A lovely King in Heaven you reign
Is there any way you can remove my stain
I still count on you dear God, oh Lord I need you true
When can I update my truth, I need to love you too

Would you like to see your manuscript become a book?

If you are interested in becoming a PublishAmerica author, please submit your manuscript for possible publication to us at:

acquisitions@publishamerica.com

You may also mail in your manuscript to:

**PublishAmerica
PO Box 151
Frederick, MD 21705**

www.publishamerica.com

CPSIA information can be obtained at www.ICGtesting.com
Printed in the USA
BVOW010200211011

274200BV00001B/117/P